What's My Who?

What's My Who?

Rediscover who you were born to be,
And what you were born to do.

Mark L. Dayton

Edited by

Jacob W. Dayton

© 2021 Timpanogos Publishing, LLC
Orem, UT

Copyright © 2021 Timpanogos Publishing

All rights reserved. No part of this publication may be reproduced, photocopied or transmitted in any form or by any means, including photocopying, recording or other electronic or mechanical methods, stored in a retrieval system or by any means shared or distributed without the prior written permission of the publisher, except in the case of brief quotations embodied in critical reviews and certain other noncommercial uses permitted by copyright law. For permission requests, write to the publisher, addressed "Attention: Permissions Coordinator," at the address below.

Timpanogos Publishing
548 E 1640 N
Orem, UT 84097
www.timpanogospublishing.com

Ordering Information:

Quantity sales: Special discounts are available on quantity purchases by corporations, associations and other third parties. For details, contact the publisher at the address above.

Printed in the United States of America

ISBN 978-1-7322363-1-8

Editor: Jacob W. Dayton
Cover art: Cynthia Dayton
Design: Varvara Jones
Cover photo:

First Edition

To Cynthia, for unfailing belief in me and unwavering encouragement, critical questioning and input, and artistic finishing touches.

To Jacob, for insightful editing and invaluable clarification of concepts and ideas, and creative fun and sparkle.

Most especially, to anyone with the courage to look inside and rediscover their true Who, and live it as a gift to the world.

Table of Contents

Introduction	1
Part 1 — What's a Who?	9
Chapter 1 — Who Before Why	11
Chapter 2 — Alignment	23
Chapter 3 — What My Who Is and Isn't	33
Part 2 — Rediscovering My Who	41
Chapter 4 — The Road to UnTrue and Rediscovery	43
Chapter 5 — The Journey Into Who	55
Part 3 — What's Stopping You?	77
Chapter 6 — A Case Study	79
Chapter 7 — So, What's Stopping You?	93
Chapter 8 — Unshakable Who + Heart of a Lion	111
Epilogue	117

The day you were born, the world changed. The day you die, the world will change again.

The quality of the space between those two infinitely important events will largely depend on how clearly you rediscover, accept and live true to who you were born to be — your true Who.

Mark L. Dayton

Introduction

What's My Who?

Introduction

I believe every person born to this world is unique. We are each different, with unique talents and insights. We each have a unique role to play, a gift to give and reason for being here, when and where we are.

When an ancient patriarch was told his seed (descendants) would be as the sands of the sea, it was both prophetic and literal. Now, billions of people later, it turns out that people and sand have a lot in common.

If you take a walk on the beach, scoop up a handful of sand and stare at it, you might not see much of anything remarkable. Sand is sand – it all looks the same, right? But one handful of sand contains approximately 400,000 grains of sand. Put it under a microscope, and you discover a myriad of different sizes, shapes and colors[1]. In fact, scientists tell us that no two grains of sand are the same in the world. That is a mind-boggling concept, when you think of all the sand on all the beaches and dunes and deserts in the world. And every grain is totally unique.

---

[1] Check out these amazing images of sand grains under the microscope: http://sandgrains.com/Sand-Grains-Gallery.html

The same concept is true of people. From the study of biology and genetics, as far as what is known, no two people have ever been identically the same on this planet, nor will another exact copy be born. About 107 billion[2] of us have joined the journey on this earth since we began, each slightly different in their own special way.

You *Can* Change the World

It's literally true that the day you were born, the world changed. The stage was set for you to impact the world in the way only you can. Large or small, thousands or few, no one else can touch others with your same influence.

That contribution requires only one thing: that we stand in the power and clarity of our own unique Who: Who we were born to be and what we were born to do. Without shame. Without fear. With clarity and conviction, enthusiasm and joy.

That's not easy to do. In the shaping and molding of our formative years (psychologists call it domestication),

---

[2] https://www.prb.org/howmanypeoplehaveeverlivedonearth/

most of us lose sight of our true who, our true purpose. But it's still there. We don't lose it — just lose sight of it.

Rediscovering, accepting and stepping into our true Who is one of the most exciting journeys in life. For many people it's like taking off the blindfold or coming out of a fog into the sunshine. Life has deeper meaning and purpose. Our daily work, regardless of how menial, is more purposeful and fulfilling. Each of us is able to set clear goals and directions for life that take us to places and relationships we may not have imagined, but that feel natural and right — like coming home.

I say rediscovering because it's not finding, discovering for the first time or creating. It's rediscovering what's already there, what's always been there, waiting to blossom and bless your corner of the world with your unique brand of Who.

Some people liken this rediscovery experience to standing on a mountaintop. It's exhilarating, empowering and freeing. Things seem to be in better perspective and balance. You have a clear view of the landscape all around, the path that got you to the top, and the possible routes for moving on. You are filled with ambition, enthusiasm and commitment.

Introduction

And then you come back down. Life gets busy and messy. The mountaintop vision gets a little cloudy. It's harder to remember with clarity the enthusiasm for the new direction you were setting out on. Without extra effort, it's easy to slip back into the pre-mountaintop ways of thinking and acting.

But, you're never really the same. Having experienced the vista of that peak, you will always have a clearer vision of who you are and what your true potential is. That is always with you, and can become a powerful guiding force in your life.

This book is intended to guide you to that rediscovery experience, and to begin to see your own path forward toward realizing your core purpose. That part of the journey can often be fairly rapid and spontaneous.

Living and moving consistently toward it is a longer, more involved process. In the book I offer some initial guidance on moving forward and dealing with some of the resistance that may be encountered. But the more detailed discussion of living the reality of your Who is the subject of another work.

So, let's get started. Your true Who is waiting. I invite you to join the journey of rediscovery. It will make all the difference.

Part 1

What's a Who?

Chapter 1

Who Before Why

For half a decade I struggled to find my Why. At the time, 'finding your Why' had burst on the scene as the magic elixir of business and even personal success. As the fervor spread, companies I worked with were all frantically drafting their 'why' statements and encouraging employees, partners, suppliers and distributors to do the same.

The logic was compelling: people don't flock to buy from a company that markets its What. They are intrigued and engaged by a company's Why. Great companies lead with Why. The classic example is Apple vs. an average computer company.

The average computer company starts with what: "We make computers." They then move to How: our computers are fast, have loads of memory and are user friendly; That's pretty much the pitch. They rarely get to Why.

Chapter 1 – Who Before Why

Apple on the other hand starts with why:

"In Everything we do, we believe in challenging the status quo. We believe in thinking differently." That's the why. Next they say, "The way we challenge the status quo is by making our products beautifully designed, simple to use, and user friendly." (How). "We make great computers." (What).

It made perfect sense, and the concept was truly inspiring and mind-expanding for me, especially because I sincerely wanted help sorting out my future direction and purpose. Clearly defining my Why seemed like the perfect answer for resetting the compass and restoring clear direction.

But while people all around me were happily crafting their Whys, mine never seemed to gel. I really worked at it. I went through all the exercises, the workshops, thinking deeply, asking 'why' seven times, and reflecting on the greater impact I and my company could have.

I looked at examples of other companies for inspiration. For example, a successful local business stated that their Why was to build and run schools in underserved countries in Eastern Europe. I admired the altruism as well as the focused business execution this mantra provided for them and their organization. I could tell it was something about which they were deeply passionate and driven. But it didn't seem like a Why to me; it seemed more like a mission statement.

Several times I composed something that seemed compelling and even somewhat epic. But the longer I sat with it, the less I felt like it really fit and defined my true purpose, which only added to my feelings of frustration.

I began to wonder if it was just me. Why was this so confusing, and why was it so hard to figure out? I knew I was no Steve Jobs, but anyone can figure out their Why, right?

I was pretty much ready to throw in the towel when I began to run into others who struggled as much as I did. Many people had a hard time even defining what a Why was, much less being able to craft their own personal version.

One day I came across this headline in Inc. Magazine that let me know the Why struggle was more widespread than I had thought:

"Why, Despite Simon Sinek's Best Efforts, You Still Don't Know Your Why"

Chapter 1 – Who Before Why

In the article, Bill Carmody, Founder and CEO of Trepoint, expressed frustration over his company's struggles in creating a Why that fit the company despite significant effort on the part of his executive team to articulate a powerful Why. In discussing it further with his advisors, Carmody concluded that the Why is a definition of values that drives the organization. His company's Why, therefore, was a series of mantras that his employees were to live by.

While I appreciated Carmody's contribution to the discussion, it still felt like something was missing, something deeper that held the key to clearing the confusion so many of us were experiencing.

The Breakthrough: Why This Why?

I would read other people's Whys, including my own, and no matter how compelling they sounded, at the end of the day they all still begged this fundamental question:

Why *this* Why?

Why does Apple, in all they do, think differently and challenge the status quo? Aren't there a lot of other people or companies who think differently, challenge the status quo, push boundaries, think outside the box?

Why did they come up with this Why, and why did that Why resonate so profoundly?

Two Directions

The answer to "Why *this* Why?" always goes in one of two different directions.

Explanation

The first is the explanation route. You ask, "Why *this* Why?" The answer: "Because we believe innovation and imagination drive success, or "Because we see opportunity in challenges," or "Because we are passionate about solving hunger with technology," or "Because we believe every child deserves an education," or "Because climate change starts with me," etc.

These are all wonderful aims, but each of these statements can still be challenged with "Why *this* Why?" They are not an explanation of fundamental purpose; they demand further explanation and elaboration.

Chapter 1 – Who Before Why

"It's Who We Are"

The second route emerged as I listened carefully to people's language, especially as they talked passionately about their Why. "We make great products because that's how we roll. That's who we are."

That's a powerful statement. "That's who we are." It can't be challenged. No value judgement, no justification. It just is.

The operative word in this second type of explanation is Who. Before Why is Who. Who is the starting point, the center, the core, that drives everything else.

The Crazy Ones: True Who

And then it hit me. Steve Jobs told us exactly what Apple's Who was.

In 1997, Apple Computer held just 3.3% of worldwide market share in personal computers. From heady beginnings in the 1980s, the company had recently fallen on the ropes, but hoped to make a turnaround with a suite of new products. Their unlikely champion: Steve Jobs, the formerly disgraced and controversial CEO, who they managed to pry away from Pixar Animation.

That year, Jobs narrated an iconic TV ad that told the world exactly what was at the core of Jobs' Who. Here's the script:

Here's to the crazy ones, the misfits, the rebels, the troublemakers, the round pegs in the square holes, the ones who see things differently.

They're not fond of rules. You can quote them, disagree with them, glorify or vilify them, but the only thing you can't do is ignore them because they change things.

They push the human race forward, and while some may see them as the crazy ones, we see genius.

Because the ones who are crazy enough to think that they can change the world, are the ones who do.

This statement was even crazier in 1997. The release of the iMac, the product that would ultimately lift Apple from economic doldrums into Silicon Valley stardom, was still 9 months away. Apple was on the heels of Newton, a multibillion-dollar venture into small consumer electronics that turned out to be a financial and technological fiasco, and they hadn't posted a profitable quarter in a long time.

Then the plucky new CEO comes out with this ad. He's crazy. It was crazy. And yet—it was authentically brilliant. In essence, Jobs was saying, "We *are* the crazy ones who will change the world. That's who we are at the very core. That's why we founded and work for Apple, and that's why we make products for you. That's why we're on the planet. This is what we were born to be and born to do."

That clarity of core Who drove Apple to record heights of success and to actually change the world in a nontrivial way. At the time of this printing, Apple is worth at least $1.3 trillion, more than the GDP of Mexico and 2% of total US market capitalization. *That* is crazy.

Before Why: Who

Putting Who at the core, here's how the revised model looks:

What's My Who?

Before Why: Who

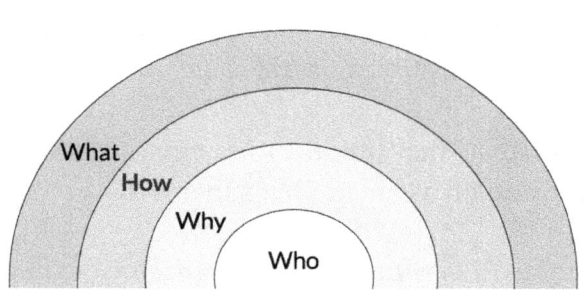

This insight is at the heart of all the previous discussion. It's actually much more than an insight. Who you are drives everything else and gives purpose and direction to why, how and what you do.

Plugging in the Apple example, everything falls into place:

Before Why: Who (Apple example)

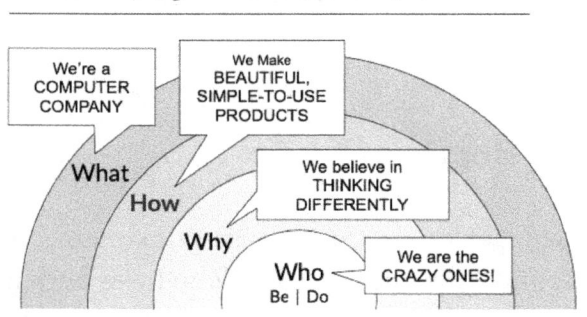

Chapter 1 – Who Before Why

At their center, Apple people are the crazy ones who will change the world. That's Who they are. No debate, no challenge, no justification. It just is.

Because of that, they think differently, challenge the status quo and break rules. That's their Why.

Because of that, they make products that are beautifully designed, simple to use, and user friendly.

What do they sell? Computers (and today phones and other devices) that are compelling and will change your life. It all lines up.

With a clear understanding of your Who, everything else falls into place. Then it's easy to understand why you are passionate about specific things, or why you value or possess certain characteristics. That then drives how you go about doing what you do, and ultimately, What you choose to do.

Born To Be; Born To Do

People who get very clear on their Who often come to this profound realization: "This is who I was born to be. It's what I was born to do." That insight resonates so deeply and authentically, they know it to be true.

There's a calm assurance and confidence that confirms it's veracity. It's personalized and customized.

It just feels right. It often pops up as a suddenly clear realization.

Many people find their born-to-be an easier, more powerful way to think about their Who. Asking straight up, "What's My Who?" can seem a bit existentially intimidating. But pondering who you were born to be, and what you were born to do while traveling the journey on this planet often brings clarity, simplicity and focus.

So, who were you born to be? Let's take a deeper dive into exactly what that means and how it plays out in our lives.

Chapter 1 – Who Before Why

Chapter 2

Alignment

I invite you to go with me on a little journey. Find a comfortable place that's as quiet as possible, where you can be uninterrupted for a few minutes. Sit down, relax and close your eyes. Actually, read the rest of these instructions, and then close your eyes.

Think back on times in your life when you were truly happy. When you felt joy and fulfillment from head to toe. Maybe you were bursting at the seams, or shouting or singing at the top of your lungs. Maybe you were basking in the quiet joy of total satisfaction. But you were engulfed with the greatest joy you have experienced.

Hold that picture in your mind for a minute and savor it. Recall the details of the circumstances that led up to and surrounded that event. What were you doing? Who were you with? What were the emotions you were experiencing?

Chapter 2 – Alignment

How were you feeling about yourself, your capabilities, your possibilities? How were you feeling about your world and the future?

Now open your eyes. Regardless of the timing or circumstances of your experience, it's highly likely that at that moment in time you were closely aligned with your core who, with who you were born to be and what you were born to do.

Alignment With Your True Who

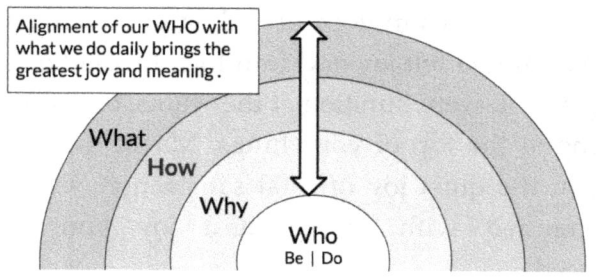

We don't think about it in those terms in the moment, but express it with phrases like, "This is everything I had hoped for," or "It doesn't get any better than this." We are often filled with a sense of deep gratitude, with a deep desire to stay in that special place.

This type of internal alignment is what produces the deepest joy and fulfillment in our lives. When what we are doing on a daily basis is in alignment with our core WHO, life is meaningful and purposeful. Time seems to fly by. Cares and worries shrink to manageable, non-threatening proportions. There is new purpose in knowing ours is a valuable contribution, and our life matters.

Greatest Gifts

Amazingly, this is also the same territory where discovery and utilization of our deepest personal gifts happens — those attributes that are unique to us, that have the greatest impact on our ability to achieve and succeed, and to impact the world for good. Even more amazingly, while moving toward utilizing our gifts, and living true to our Who, opportunities start to open that were never before imagined as possible.

I met Ellen through coaching and mentoring groups, and appreciated her insights and enthusiasm for self-introspection and self-improvement in our group meeting. I later had the opportunity to coach with her in exploring her Who.

Chapter 2 – Alignment

Ellen was an accomplished musician who was both talented and passionate about sharing her gift with the world. However, over the years she drifted away from deep involvement in music, believing that it couldn't be a serious vocation for her. She instead gravitated toward business-related ventures where she achieved a certain level of success and earned enough to pay the bills. But over time, she began to feel increasingly empty and frustrated with the path she was on.

In a moment of honest introspection she had a breakthrough insight: she was born to bring peace and comfort to people's lives through her musical gift. That's what she was born to be and what she was born to do. That realization was electrifying and deeply satisfying in a way she hadn't experienced for a long time.

As she shifted her focus, Ellen soon began to search out venues and opportunities to live her Who. It started small, with local care centers and trauma and emotional health venues where she began filling hearts and lifting spirits one song at a time. Her focus is now expanding to corporate and institutional settings. The What and How of her core purpose continue to unfold in line with her new focus.

Misalignment

Now close your eyes again, and think of times when things weren't going so well. Maybe things seemed a little off, out of control, unmanageable. Maybe things were really tough. Perhaps money was tight, relationships were raw, or dreams dashed.

What were you doing at the time? Who were you with? What were the emotions you were experiencing? How did you feel about yourself, your capabilities and your future?

You may have felt confused or frustrated about the circumstances that brought you to that point. You may have used phrases like, "What am I supposed to do?" or "I don't get it. How could this happen?"

Chances are high that at that time, you weren't closely aligned with your core Who. It may have been a time you were searching for meaning or understanding in life, or a time of pressing decisions and directional changes. But things just felt one-off, out of balance.

Alignment With Your True Who

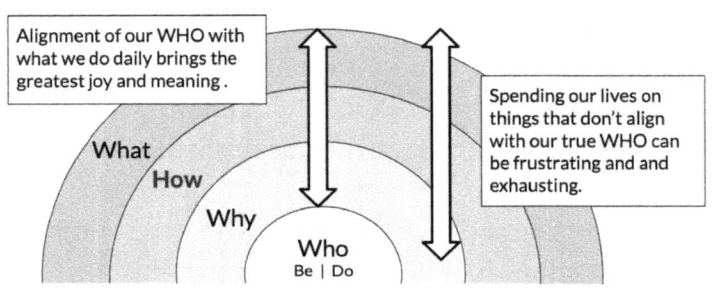

When we're fuzzy on our Who, it's easy to engage in things that are out of alignment with our core. It quickly becomes drudgery. Feeling trapped, uninterested, confused, and meaningful encounters seem shallow or short-lived. We may even start to question more fundamental things, like, "What's the point with what I do?" and "Does my life really matter?"

Instead of energized and excited to get going, we find ourselves slogging through and wondering if this is as good as it gets. Deep inside there is a desire to believe it must, but our vision is blocked.

When I first met Jake, I was impressed. Very smart guy, good looking, talented, friendly. Good family man, great with his kids. Reasonably successful in his career, though not setting any records.

And yet, there was something off. As I looked at him I said, "He's super talented, capable, socially astute. He has every reason to be highly successful, happy and enthusiastic. But something is missing. Something is askew. I can't quite put my finger on it, but I can sense it."

I soon learned that Jake was a highly motivated entrepreneur who dreamed of working for himself and building his own business, but was stuck in a company job where he felt trapped, unappreciated and severely under compensated.

The more we talked, the more it became obvious that he was fuzzy on his own Who. The entrepreneur that was at his core was totally out of sync with the corporate job he felt compelled to continue. His life was drudgery. His marriage and family suffered. His income suffered. His happiness, confidence and optimism suffered.

Over a short period of time, I worked with Jake in helping him rediscover and embrace his Who. He came to realize that he was born to be an entrepreneur, to build and create with his brilliant mind and talents. He soon quit his job, started his own business and doubled his income. I watched in amazement as his marriage and family life flourished, his confidence continued to grow, and his laughter and love of life skyrocketed.

What's My Who?

Chapter 2 – Alignment

Chapter 3

What My Who Is and Isn't

Understanding your Who and being able to clearly see it and live it are often two very different things.

Your Who — who you were born to be and what you were born to do — is a deeply personal and intrinsic part of who you are. But it's not always simple to identify and articulate. Often there are blocks to our true Who and sometimes questions concerning our own intuition and inspiration.

To help you clarify the image of your Who, here are some guidelines on what a Who is and isn't. Keep in mind that your Who is deeply personal and specific to you. There is no right or wrong — only what's true for you. However, these guidelines may help clarify your rediscovery process.

Also, keep in mind that the subconscious mind is an active participant in defining our Who. Because it tends to operate, clear communications and images, some of these guidelines align with addressing the power of that part of our psyche.

What My Who IS

One short, simple statement. "I am…" Clarity comes from a statement that is fairly short, clear and concise. You may be surprised at how short and clear a Who can be. (Think of, "we're the crazy ones" for Apple).

An Image. How you picture yourself. The characteristics you envision. What you do, who you do it with/for. Find or draw a picture that captures the image in your mind.

A Strong Emotion. You will feel it deeply, often with unexpected emotion. It's not uncommon for tears and strong emotion to accompany rediscovering your Who. This is a good indication that you're on the right track.

Highly Personal. It is unique to you and you alone. Comparing other people's Who can be instructive as to the range of possibilities. But your Who is unique to you and you alone. There is no right or wrong. If yours is vastly different, hurrah for you!

Something You Sense. You don't figure it out or think it. You feel it. You sense it. You know it is true intrinsically.

Often a First Impression. When you are exploring these ideas, often the first impressions that come to you are closest to the truth. The subconscious is direct and clear. Overthinking and stressing about it usually only serves to cloud the picture.

Multi-Layered. The longer you work with it, you may discover that there are multiple deeper levels of understanding and insight that weren't at first apparent.

What My Who Is NOT

A Title (teacher, doctor, executive, etc.) This is your What. (See Chapter 6 for an example).

A Role We Play. This might include coach, volunteer, block captain or other positions we fill.

A Long Paragraph. Best is one short, clear, precise statement. From the heart.

A Long List of Characteristics. This is usually aspirational head-talk. A short list of characteristics is great and usually tied to strong emotions about your Who.

A 'Can', 'Ought' or 'Will Be'. Your true WHO is 'I am…' Statements like "I can help people around the world…" or "I will be instrumental in…" are not who you are.

Chapter 3 - What My Who Is and Isn't

They are perceived aspirations as to what you wish you could be.

A Generality. A generality is something like "I am a child of God" or "...of the Universe" or "a valued member of the human race." These are immensely important statements of deeply held beliefs about self. They are to be honored and treated with the utmost respect.

That said, they are more of a jumping off point rather than an end point. They aren't specifically who you are because you are unique in all the universe!

It's like making the football, basketball, lacrosse, softball...team. Or orchestra, chorus, play, etc. You work hard. You practice. You sacrifice. You try out. And you make the cut. You're on the team! The coach says, "Congratulations. You made the team." Making the cut is a major accomplishment, to be sure.

But it's about a lot more than just making the team, as important as that is. As a member of the team, you play a specific part, position or role. It's specific to you. And although there are others who play a similar role (right tackle, 1st flute, etc.) no one fills that role exactly as you do. You bring your own creativity, insight, flair and interpretation that makes your contribution unique. It is capable of influencing and touching others as only you can.

So beyond making the team, your Who includes specifics around your born-to-be that are unique to the role you play. And it's not about same-ness, different-ness, or uniqueness. It's not about comparison with someone else, and how they play a similar role. The real test is alignment: alignment with the true born-to-be in your heart.

Permanently Unchangeable. Once you clearly understand your Who and start down that path, your understanding and interpretation of that insight will likely refine and sharpen over time. These won't be major deviations, but refinements that fit with a current life stage or insight.

Something You Think or Figure Out. It's something you sense to be true. You know, but don't know why you know. You just know it's true.

Destructive or Hurtful. No human being was born to be destructive, hateful, prejudiced, vengeful or damaging to others. This is *not* anyone's Who. Period. We came to this planet endowed with intrinsically loving natures. Anyone who says they were born to hack into bank accounts and steal money or enslave other human beings is confused or deceived.

Hone It, Not Overthink It

Clarity of your Who will come over time and as you continue to ponder it and start seeing it in action. You may have additional insights that will help hone it down even further. But it's not something to stress over, doubt or continually re-draft and refine. It *is* possible to overthink it.

Now that we've explored what a Who is and isn't, we'll take a journey into the process of actually rediscovering it.

What's My Who?

Chapter 3 - What My Who Is and Isn't

Part 2

Rediscovering My Who

Chapter 4

The Road to UnTrue and Rediscovery

Every being on this planet came to earth with a purpose. Everything that exists has purpose. If it doesn't have purpose, it ceases to exist. The fact that you exist means you have a purpose for being here.
Each of our lives started with a life purpose, our born-to-be, planted in our hearts and perfectly aligned with our Why, How and What. Everything was clear, simple and congruous — but our awareness was low.

This life purpose stays with us throughout our journey on the planet. It's not something you grow into or out of. It can mature and refine as we grow, but the core purpose is unique to each of us as a constant identity throughout life.

Very early on, our perception of our Who is clear and unbiased, and what we do is very much in sync with our core.

Alignment With Your True Who

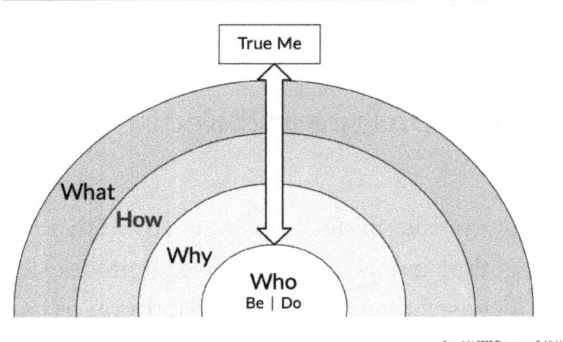

The Journey to UnTrue

In our life journey, things start to get a little fuzzy around our Who and Why, moving away from clearly seeing and believing the true Who at our core, and instead creating a perception of ourselves that is rarely an accurate reflection of the clear view of our inner who. Once out of alignment, we say and do things that don't resonate and can leave us confused and frustrated.

How does this happen?

Over time, most of us go searching for our identity outside of ourselves and begin looking to others to define us and help us feel a sense of worth.

It happens through a combination of the influences and expectations of well-meaning caretakers, teachers, friends and family, and our own needs and perceptions of what will ensure being accepted, loved and cared for.

Here are a few of the major influences that contribute to this shift:

Expectations. Well-meaning caretakers, teachers, family and friends unwittingly put expectations and judgments on us. While it's all well intentioned and often loving, no one but you knows your true born-to-be. So naturally much of the feedback you receive will be at odds with your core purpose, no matter how sincere or insightful the other person may be.

But to ensure continual approval and love of these people who are so important to us, their expectations become our own.

Need for Approval. A strong desire to be popular and included can drive us to abandon integrity to our true Who in favor of an image that is more readily accepted by a new tribe as well.

Shame. Shame follows next when expectations set by others whose approval we desire is not attained. Regardless of how far out of sync with our core Who those expectations may be, the deep desire to be accepted overrules. Shame is a powerful motivator that pushes us further from our true Who in the quest for acceptance.

Comparison. When we begin to compare and evaluate ourselves based on outside images and values, rather than our own internal WHO, it's easy to lose a sense of self. This process has been vastly accelerated through social media and online technologies that provide instant and continuous comparison and ranking of worth by likes and followers.

Negative Thoughts. It's astounding how many negative thoughts spontaneously go through our minds daily. Cognitive Behavioral Therapists have a term for it — ANTs (Automatic Negative Thoughts). According to the National Science Foundation, an average person has about 12,000 to 60,000 thoughts per day. Of those, **80%** are negative and **95%** are repetitive thoughts.

Because the subconscious is very obedient, it takes our thoughts and assembles the evidence and circumstances to make thoughts into actions that happen. By allowing our natural ANTs tendencies to take hold every day, the majority of our thoughts and efforts will be centered on negativity and what we're incapable of doing and being, rather than living true to who we actually are and what we are actually capable of doing.

Dark Whispers. Beyond internally generated ANTs, there are negative or destructive thoughts that clearly come from somewhere outside of ourselves. These are ideas we never would have come up with on our own, even in the subconscious. I call them dark whispers, because they are negative, dark and personally destructive to our perception and acceptance of our true selves.

Power, Money. The quest for recognition through money and/or power can push us to bury core true Who characteristics and actions in favor of those that will enhance the accolades these two powerful forces can deliver.

Over years of experience and repetition, these emotionally charged skewed perceptions become beliefs, wired into the subconscious and layered with miles of repetitious wiring that become neural super highways. Beliefs then become our reality.

So, rather than a 'true me' wired to a true Who, there is a fuzzy Who wired to a skewed perception, and also separated by a strong wall of shame, expectation, and gloom (negative thoughts, comparison, dark whispers, power and money).

Fuzzy Who

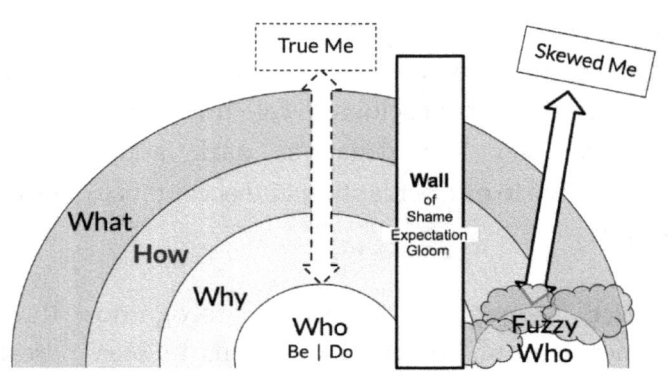

Rediscover vs Find, Discover, Make Up, Invent, Copy

In this process of coming back to your true Who, it's necessary to rediscover rather than discover, or find, because the born-to-be you came with never left. It's always been an intrinsic part of you, and always will be. With a clear view, rediscovering what was always there is possible.

This is important to keep in mind. Some people want to create a great Who for themselves, or perhaps take ideas from other great people and compile a wonderfully aspirational purpose for being on the planet. Like creating a strong vision or mission statement.

Your Who can't be created or invented, and doesn't need to be. It's just there, waiting to be rediscovered.

Don't Figure It Out — Sense It

While it can be thought about, rediscovering your Who is ultimately a sensory experience as much as a cognitive experience. You don't need to plan it, draft it, figure it out, or invent it. You sense it in the soulful self.

It's the process of quieting the mind and soul, and connecting deep inside. It will take some work and introspection, and perhaps a number of attempts over a period of time. But when you connect with your core Who, it rings true. It feels absolutely right. You know it's true and it's you. A flood of emotion often accompanies the experience. It strikes deeply in the soul with calm, reassuring clarity.

It's often short and quite simple.

Some people may challenge, "That's it? That's your Who?" Others may ask, "Why is that your Who?" The answer is, "It just IS. It's who I am. It's Who I was born to be." It doesn't have to be defended or justified. It doesn't have to be explained. It just is. It's you.

In a moment you'll be given the opportunity to think about your Who in a way you may not have contemplated for some time, if ever. Move into the experience, trust your instincts and connect with your true Who.

The Role of Inspiration

The rediscovery process relies on understanding how our mind and emotions interact in this introspective journey, but also understanding the role of inspiration and tuning into this powerful source of insight.

In reality, inspiration explains the unexplainable. Every person on this planet experiences strokes of inspiration and insight that are totally outside of themselves. They are flashes of illumination that come as guiding input, often when we need it most.

We sometimes call them God-given gifts — and with good reason. They can't be explained by brain science or cognitive theory. Yet they are real and powerful. They are part of what makes each of us unique and vitally important on this planet.

I know of scientists who get to certain points in their research and hit a dead end. They get stuck. And suddenly, they have a stroke of inspiration, a new insight on how to move forward. It's from totally outside of themselves, and not explainable by any earthly mechanism. And yet it's real.

Other people find wisdom and insight through meditation, introspection, prayer, faith and mindfulness. In quiet moments of reflection, ideas and insights can come to us that resonate deeply and that are known to be intrinsically true for us.

In a way, rediscovering our Who is a journey in getting unstuck. When willing, we can access the awesome power of the conscious and subconscious mind and combine it with the wisdom and insight of inspiration to understand our true Who in brilliant new ways.
It's a choice. And the most meaningful personal insights come to those who choose both internal and supernal wisdom.

Don't Panic — Rediscovery May Take Time

Some people may believe they aren't the 'touchy-feely' type to look inside and clarify their Who. Others sincerely give it a go, but don't feel that they've gotten to that core Who that really resonates with them.

Chapter 4 – The Road to UnTrue and Rediscovery

Does that mean you'll be a failure, miserable and frustrated your whole life? Don't panic. The full extent of rediscovery may take some time. We're each at a different point in our journey, our openness to new ideas, and our need for clarity and deeper meaning.

Actually, many people find great success, achievement, and wealth without rediscovering their Who, or in doing things they weren't born to do. But the closer you get to it, the greater the opportunity is to impact your own life, those you love, and ultimately the world in the most meaningful way that will bring the greatest satisfaction and fulfillment. It will be the contribution that is most uniquely you.

The flip side of this is that by choosing to stay in the place of shame, expectation and all the rest, we are actually living someone else's Who, not our own. We're living the Who they expect and want from us, not the one that's unique to us.

It can be tricky to unravel, but more insight and clarity are always available. Be patient. And above all, trust your insight and instinct. No matter how thickly layered or convoluted our self-perception may be, our true Who yearns to re-emerge and be authentically expressed. It's the chance each of us deserves.

What's My Who?

Chapter 4 – The Road to UnTrue and Rediscovery

Chapter 5

The Journey into Who

Let's go on another little imaginary journey. Find a place that's as quiet and comfortable as possible. Relax and clear your mind of all present worries and distractions, and just let yourself enjoy the story.

Angie was a department manager for a store that was part of a large chain retailer. She really loved clothes and loved helping customers find exactly what they were looking for. She especially enjoyed working with women who came into the store wanting to look beautiful, but not believing they really could, and especially not at a price they could afford. Her greatest source of satisfaction was seeing the look on the face of a woman who walked out with a dress or outfit that boosted her confidence and belief that she was beautiful and worthwhile.

Angie's boss, Jen was constantly pressuring her to upsell customers on more expensive items and push lines of clothes that the store highlighted rather than an individualized approach. But because Angie had a real knack for helping customers find that perfect outfit, Jan made her work far too many nights, weekends, and holidays. The long hours were a

Chapter 5 – The Journey into Who

drag on her social life as well, making it a challenge to build more meaningful friendships and dating relationships.

Though Angie liked her job, she didn't really see herself doing it her whole life. She knew something was missing, but didn't exactly know what else she'd rather do her whole life. Well, that wasn't quite true – there was one thing, but that was an impractical fantasy she'd had as a teenager, and she'd be embarrassed if anyone knew about it, even now.

One night, after a long day of demanding customers, bumbling associates, and snarky remarks from Jen, Angie went home and flopped down on her bed, too drained and exhausted to do anything. Tears moistened her face as she thought of the increasingly meaningless but comforting certainty of her day-to-day life, and her inability to find much joy in what she was doing. These thoughts swam through her head as she closed her eyes...

Suddenly, Angie's eyes snapped open. She looked around and found herself standing entirely alone in an unfamiliar landscape. The area was completely flat, with no mountains, hills, trees, bushes, or other interruptions to her view of the horizon as far as she could see in every direction. The sun was just setting, bathing the landscape in a warm, purple-orange glow. Directly in front of her was a large protrusion of rock jutting up about 20 feet.

Not knowing what to do or where she was, Angie decided to climb the outcropping of rock and take a look around. Maybe she could see some city lights from up there and make it back before dawn. She couldn't be that far from civilization, could she?

After a short scramble, with the help of a short loose stick she found along the way, Angie pulled herself to the top, breathing hard, and flopped on her back, splaying her arms and hands as she rested.

After regaining her breath, she propped herself up on one elbow and quickly scanned the horizon. No sign of a city light or any type of civilization as far as the eye could see. Confused, she plopped onto her back again.

As she continued resting, Angie stared up into the night sky. From up here, she had an unobstructed view of a glorious expanse of stars popping out overhead as the last lingering daylight was swallowed up in darkness.

The temperature was perfect — one of those nights where you can't tell if it's warm or cool. The sky overhead was brilliant with stars that pierced the blackness of space with a variety of shapes and glittering patterns. Directly above, the Milky Way painted a vivid swath of light and color from one horizon to the other.

Chapter 5 – The Journey into Who

As she took in this beautiful scene, she was filled with awe and wonder, gazing back millions of years at the light of trillions of stars from distant galaxies.

Angie absentmindedly fiddled with the stick still in her hand. Suddenly, she heard someone say, "Ouch!"

She jumped to her feet, heart racing. "Who's there?" Without thinking, Angie had brandished the stick in her hand, holding it out like a sword. She looked this way and that, but saw no one. Suddenly, the stick spoke.

"That was me!" exclaimed the stick. "Be careful how you wave me around." Angie blinked at the stick in surprise.

"A talking stick?" Angie said.

"Actually, I'm not a stick," replied the stick. "I'm a wand."

Angie stared at the wand for a moment, wrapping her mind around what she was hearing. "So I can wave you and cast spells and do magic?" Angie asked.

"Actually, I'm a specialized wand," the wand clarified. "No spells or magic, but I can grant you three wishes, if you choose."

"Wow, three wishes!" exclaimed Angie, thinking of the possibilities. No more Jen – No more unhappy customers, no

more nights and weekends — no more meaningless relationships — she could just wish them all away!

"Before you choose," the wand clarified, "I can only grant three specific types of wishes. They're still amazing, but I only have powers in three specific areas. Trust me, you won't be disappointed."

"All right, I understand," said Angie. Even with restrictions, three free wishes from a magic wand sounded pretty enticing.

"The first wish is that you will be granted relief from all your current cares and worries for the next 60 days. No worries about job, or money, or relationships, or other responsibilities. They will all be taken care of. You won't have to think about what you say or do, because all your needs will be met. Do you wish this?"

Angie looked at the wand, considering. That did actually sound pretty nice. No work, no worries, no one judging or criticizing her for 60 days? "Yes," said Angie. "I wish that."

"Then wave me like you mean it, and repeat the words," the wand encouraged.

Angie nodded. As she raised the wand, she noticed the end starting to glow, and as she waved it overhead, a bright light suddenly burst out, splitting the dark night sky. "I wish that

Chapter 5 – The Journey into Who

I will be granted relief from all my current responsibilities for 60 days."

The light from the wand intensified, and the wand exclaimed, "Wish granted!"

Angie suddenly felt a weight lift off her shoulders, and a sense of relief and relaxation washed through her whole body. She gave a little sigh of relief.

"Wonderful," the wand replied. "Now for the second wish. If you choose to wave me again, you will be granted the ability to do anything you want. It can be a one shot deal, to just do one big thing. Or, you can choose to be doing something for as long as you want. Anything you want, for as long as you want."

"Do you choose to wave me?"

Angie hesitated. This was a pretty fantastic wish. She thought about all the exotic places she could go or amazing things she could do. Anything she'd ever dreamed of! But then, suddenly, another thought popped into her head. It was that teenage fantasy she had always been a little embarrassed about, but that seemed to always be there nagging at the back of her mind. With all her cares and worries temporarily gone, maybe this was the time to try it out.

I've always loved clothes, but I've always secretly wanted to design clothes, not just sell them," Angie started.

"Is that your wish?" the wand queried as it began to glow again.

"Yes, that's my wish," Angie replied, *grasping the wand tightly and waving it energetically overhead, light streaming in all directions. "I wish to be a fashion designer!"* she exclaimed. *"But not just any fashion designer,"* she clarified, *smiling at the wand. "This is a very specific type of wish."*

Delighted, the wand responded, "Wish granted. Tell me what you see." Before them a scene opened, and Angie began describing the events unfolding. "I'm designing clothes, but not just any clothes. I've always wanted to design clothes that would help every woman feel she is beautiful, that she is capable and enough, just the way she is. So, here I am, creating clothes that are beautiful and elegant in design, but practical and affordable for almost any woman."

"Look at that woman," Angie continued, *pointing to another area of the scene. "She never thought she could afford to buy clothes that looked beautiful on her. She always felt dumpy and out of style in the clothes that were in her budget. And there's a dress I designed. She's trying it on. It's elegant and flattering, but very affordable — not marked way up and loaded with expensive extras."*

Chapter 5 – The Journey into Who

"Look at her face, "Angie continued. *"She's so happy and feels so good about herself — like she's worthwhile, as well as being a good money manager!"*

"And what are you feeling at this moment?" asked the wand, looking back toward Angie.

"The deepest satisfaction I can imagine," said Angie. "A combination of elation, fulfillment and gratitude. Like I'm doing something really useful in the world with my skills and passion. The fulfillment of a lifelong dream. Like this is what I was always meant to do."

"That's a beautiful wish," the wand replied as the scene in front of them faded back into the dark, starry sky.

Angie was quiet for a few moments as she contemplated what had just transpired. "What could the third wish contain that could possibly be better than this?" she thought.

"Let's move on to the third wish." the wand broke into her thoughts, "That is, if you still choose the third wish…"

"Oh yes, definitely," Angie replied.

"The third wish is the grandest of all," the wand began. Angie was still wondering what could outdo her first two wishes. "If you choose this third wish," the wand continued, "you will be

granted the ability to be anything you choose to be. No limitations. It can be anything you've always wanted to be."

Angie was momentarily stunned. Anything she wanted to be! Her mind began racing, thinking of all the famous, iconic people she could be like, the positions, power and notoriety that were all hers with one wave of the wand. After cycling through a seemingly endless parade of possibilities, suddenly everything cleared, and one simple idea bubbled up and took center stage: that nagging fantasy was back. But this time she knew there was something more, something deeper that was at the heart of that vision she had long ago that had never left her.

She took a deep breath. "Okay. I'm ready."

"Here we go!" replied the wand."

Angie grasped the wand firmly, and after a moment of hesitation, circled it rapidly overhead, light streaming in a symmetrical pattern above her.

A scene again opened in front of them, and Angie spontaneously began describing what they were witnessing. "Deep inside, I've always wanted to ultimately be like a beacon or lighthouse in the dark to inspire womens' confidence and belief in themselves and their own unique power and beauty. Not to set myself up as superior or better than, but to

Chapter 5 – The Journey into Who

inspire them and assure them that they are naturally beautiful, capable and valued."

The scene shifted and Angie continued. "Sometimes I might be designing, or speaking, or teaching, or being interviewed, or coaching one-on-one. Maybe something I have written or said or designed will impact a woman in a way that will give her the courage to stand a little taller, and believe that she has something valuable to give."

Angie continued, "In my ideal world, many women look to me for inspiration, and discover their own confidence and unique gifts."

"So, you're a beacon or icon of hope and confidence for women wanting to believe more deeply in themselves," the wand summarized. "Is that it?"

"It sounds a little crazy," Angie started slowly, "but yes. I think that's who I was born to be."

"Discovering and claiming who you were born to be isn't the least bit crazy," the wand assured. "It's the deepest wish of the heart, and the one I'm always most anxious to grant to those with the courage to explore and express it honestly."

"Now, repeat the wish," the wand encouraged, "just to make sure it fully takes."

"I wish to be a beacon of hope and confidence for women to believe in themselves," Angie repeated slowly and firmly.

In one last burst of light the wand exclaimed, "Wish granted!"

The scene again faded and Angie immediately felt a deep sense of peace wash over her — a calm, joyful, grounded feeling of completeness. No doubt, no fear, no confusion. "I feel like I just came home after a long, tiring and frustrating trip," she explained. "Like this is where I belong; where I've always belonged."

"You are home," the wand confirmed. "And now you have eyes to see more clearly the way ahead for living true to who you now are — who you were always meant to be."

Angie's heart swelled with gratitude as she gazed back up at the blaze of stars overhead and contemplated the three great gifts she has just received. She couldn't have imagined the magnitude of what had been granted to her.

She held the wand at eye level, just in case wands enjoy looking at the stars as well. After a few minutes of silence, the wand broke in, "It is a beautiful sight, but our time together is coming to an end. Is there anything you'd like to ask me?"

"Just one thing," replied Angie. "How can I ever possibly thank you?"

Chapter 5 – The Journey into Who

"The best thing you can do is live true to the beacon you are, and to what you were meant to do," the wand replied. "The minute you start to believe this was all just some crazy dream, the magic will fade and your wishes will become nothing more than fond memories."

Angie silently nodded her understanding.

"Now, wave me one last time, and you'll be transported back to your home," the wand instructed. "I will go with you, but there will be no more wishes or conversations. Only a reminder of what transpired for you here under the stars tonight."

Angie raised the wand and slowly waved it overhead as the light streamed skyward one last time. Suddenly the world started swirling and then went dark.

Angie opened her eyes and found herself lying on the bed exactly as she had been before her excursion. She glanced around the room — everything just the same as before.

She sat up, and felt something hard under her hand. Glancing down, she saw a smooth, slender stick with a soft light still glowing from the end. Angie smiled, knowing that for her, nothing was the same.

Now It's Your Turn

This is your chance to take a journey similar to Angie's and look inside at the possibility of rediscovering who you were truly born to be.

Imagine yourself transported to the same remote outcropping under the expanse of stars, thousands of miles from any civilization. It's a warm, quiet night, and you feel completely relaxed.

Suddenly, you encounter the wand, which grants you the same three wishes. As you think through each of the three wishes, capture your thoughts, images and feelings in the blanks below.

My 3 Wishes

Wish #1

You are granted relief from all your current cares and worries for the next 60 days. No worries about job, or money, or relationships, or other responsibilities. They will all be taken care of. You won't have to think about what you say or do, because all your needs will be met."

3 Emotions I feel:

1.

2.

3.

Wish #2

You are granted the ability to do anything you want. It can be a one shot deal, to just do one big thing. Or, you can choose to do something for as long as you want. Anything you want, for as long as you want."

What I do or am doing:

What does it look like? Three sights that describe what I am doing:

1.

2.

3.

What sounds do I hear? Three sounds associated with what I am doing:

1.

2.

3.

What do I smell? Three aromas that waft up to me:

1.

2.

3.

Chapter 5 – The Journey into Who

Who I am doing it with, or for:

What impact does it have (on me, on my loved ones, on my community, etc.)?

How do I feel? Three emotions I am experiencing:

1.

2.

3.

Wish #3

You are granted the ability to be anything you choose to be. No limitations. It can be anything you've always wanted to be.

How I describe myself in one short sentence* (3-10 words):

"I am...

"

The image I see. Here's a rough sketch of the scene that describes me:

How I feel. Three emotions I am experiencing:

1.

2.

3.

The difference I make. This is the impact I now make in the world:

Now, take a deep breath and let this all sink in. Allow some time to process what you have just experienced.

Born to Be, Born to Do

Now go back to the information you filled in above, and next to Wish #2 write "Born to Do." and next to Wish #3 write "Born to Be."

You can summarize what you are doing and what you chose to be in this chart:

Journey Into Who

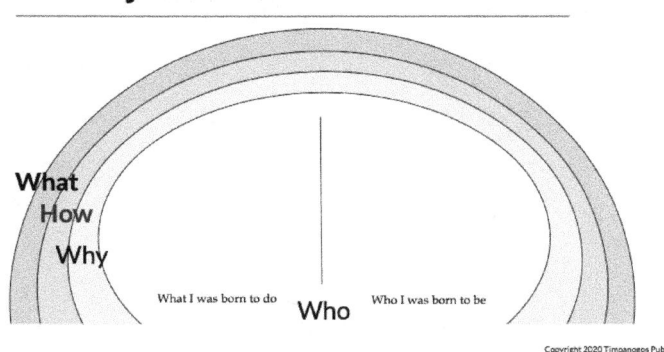

Next, read through again everything you have written, and let it sink in. Does it feel authentic and true? As crazy as it may sound, does it describe who you *really* are? Is it like the person you always secretly admired, but never imagined could be you?

Do you feel a twinge of excitement, a spontaneous smile, or maybe a giggle or even a full-on laugh as you think about this person being you?

Maybe you're experiencing a sudden, unexpected surge of emotion that makes talking momentarily challenging or perhaps a little eye leakage.

Chapter 5 – The Journey into Who

Is it easy to say, "Yes. This is who I was born to be. This is what I was born to do!"

If so, you've made the connection with your true Who, your born-to-be.

Welcome home.

*Try limiting this description to a very short phrase. It's usually the first thing that comes up when you do this exercise. It's often fairly short and simple. Whatever that first thought or impression is, write it down, no matter how simple or silly or surprising it may seem at first. You're not trying to create an award-winning Who statement here by overthinking and wordsmithing it. You are capturing the very core of who you are as it pops out of your subconscious.

What's My Who?

Chapter 5 – The Journey into Who

Part 3

What's Stopping You?

Chapter 6

A Case Study

A clearly defined Who impacts all aspects of our lives, from normal, everyday activities to major decisions regarding direction and purpose. It opens a world of possibilities, all tied to our core reason for being, and manifested in ways that best leverage our greatest gifts and abilities, and that will be of greatest benefit to those we reach out to in our lives.

Here's an example. If I ask a doctor, "What's your Who? Who were you born to be? What were you born to do on this planet?" Predictably, the response is, "I was born to be a doctor."

That's a great start, but unfortunately, "doctor" isn't a Who; it's a title, and a title is a What. Any title is: teacher, contractor, salesperson, public servant, business owner. Many people miss the opportunity of clearly understanding and connecting with their true Who because they mistakenly believe that their title, or titles, are their Who. They aren't.

Chapter 6 - A Case Study

In fact, your What is as far from your core Who as you can get. So, let's dig a little deeper and explore the true Who of our doctor friend.

Getting to Who

Our doctor is an open-minded, introspective person committed to self-improvement. And after working through it and really digging deep inside, she comes to the realization of what her true Who is; what she was born to be: "I am a compassionate and gifted healer."

She senses it, she feels it, she knows it to be true. It can't be explained or justified. It just is. It's simple, clear, and resonates deeply — all signs that you've rediscovered your true Who.

So, a compassionate, gifted healer is what she was born to be on this planet. And compassionate healing is what she was born to do. That's her true Who. We'll put that at the core of the model like this:

True Who

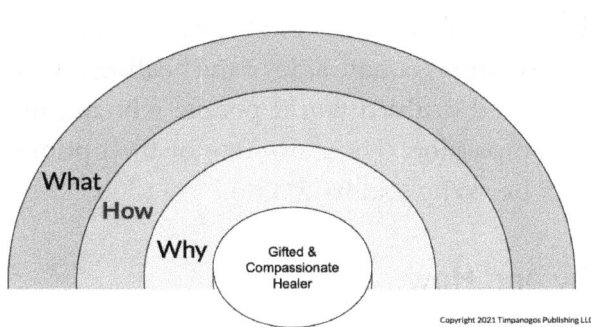

That clarity opens a world of possibilities regarding life direction and engagement. Most amazingly, it intrinsically helps fence in and guide her to those things that are most closely aligned with her core true Who, and fence out and steer her away from blind alleys and dead ends that are out of alignment with her core, and that would ultimately create stress, dissatisfaction, and less than her best performance.

Now let's look at the Why. This doctor's Why is, "I combine my intrinsic healing gift with compassionate care for astounding cures." That's pretty powerful.

Next is How. At each level the possibilities continue to expand. There are many How options. She could train for a lower-volume, higher-interaction specialty where added attention and compassion could positively impact outcomes. She could own her own private practice. She could form a group with other specialists who share a similar passion and gift. She could really dial up the compassionate side of the healing gift and go to underserved or third world people who are most in need of compassion. These are few of the options that align with her Why and true Who.

Why and How

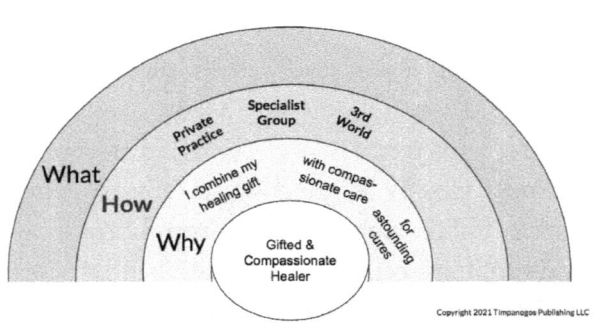

Finally, depending on the How selected, the What falls out. Yes, she's a doctor. But rather than being a non-clinical medical director for a pharmaceutical company, this doctor chose to be a partner in a group practice that focuses on pushing the boundaries for adopting new and innovative treatments for accelerated healing through compassionate care.

Aligned What

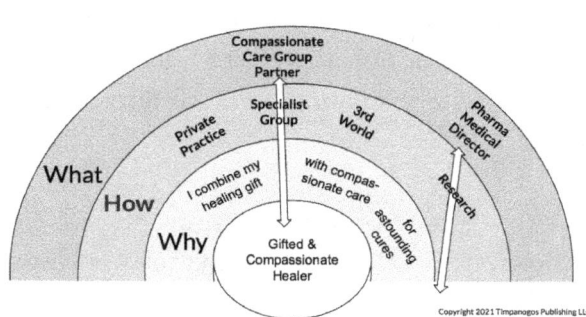

The result is a doctor who can't wait to get to the clinic each day and see patients. She feels a deep sense of purpose in her work, and knows that what she does makes a difference in the world. While at times exhausted, she doesn't experience the burnout so many colleagues are increasingly confronted with.

And most importantly, her patients are served with the finest, most attentive, cutting-edge compassionate care available, with outcomes that match.

All Roles Aligned

This doctor also finds great fulfillment and success in other areas of life as she is clearly aligned with her true Who. Her connection with that compassionate, healing core guides her to serve on a nonprofit board and work with a humanitarian project with other doctors providing care to third world countries. She is also contemplating serving in her local municipal government, where healing of a different nature is needed.

And clarity of that connection brings special insight, compassion and healing to family relationships and guidance to children during difficult or challenging times.

Possibilities

The expanded number of possibilities aligned with our core is truly thrilling when we can clearly see and articulate our true Who. It's like a flashlight shining on a path of possibilities for us to follow and choose from.

What-to-Who Map

Here's an exercise to try. Create a rainbow chart for yourself similar to those earlier in this chapter, and label it with Who in the center, and Why, How and What moving outward. Next, write in a few of your titles or roles in the What sector. This could be your job or career title, and others that are important to you, such as parent, friend, board member, volunteer, etc.

Include hobbies or other interests you are passionate about and give your time and energy to. You could put golfer, quilter, gardener, marathoner, artist, video gamer...whatever is a major priority in your life.

Finally, write in one or two of the options you may have been considering lately for allocating additional time and focus. Maybe you're considering additional part-time work, or you've been invited to join a club or team; or perhaps you're considering taking lessons to perfect that talent that has always been a lingering desire. Regardless of where you are in the decision process, write in those you are considering.

Now write your Who in the center of the chart. It may spill over a bit, but write down the full Who you rediscovered earlier — or that you intrinsically knew. If you're still not sure you've fully clarified it, write down what you think it might be at this point. Get as close as you can to it, and stay open for further insight as you work your map.

Chapter 6 - A Case Study

Mapping

Now pick a role or hobby or decision from the What segment and start working your way toward the center. First ask, "How am I fulfilling this role or activity?" While it may seem obvious, write down the response. It's important to have each response in place to see the patterns emerge.

Next go to Why. What is the principal reason you are engaged in this activity? What are the outcomes you are experiencing or expecting?

Finally move to Who. Check the alignment of this chain with your core Who. Would you need to re-write your Who to make it fit? Or does it naturally fit and resonate with what you are doing, how and why?

As you move through each one, you may find greater and lesser degrees of fit with your true Who. For each one that is off or slightly out, ask the question, "Is there something I could change here to bring this more closely into alignment with my core?"

Stay open to options and inspiration. You may see an insight you hadn't previously realized about how to engage in a particular activity or role, or perhaps adjust your approach so that your Why for doing it is more meaningful.

There may be roles and activities that are clearly disconnected from you true Who. These are the ones to focus on and ponder. They are items you are giving you time and your life to, yet they may be out of alignment with who you are at your core. Give serious consideration to the purpose they serve, and why you give a portion of your life to them.

Try writing a modified Why and Who for these items that better fits them. As you look at this altered alignment, you may find that you've discovered one of those Whos that isn't really your own — that it's an expectation or belief you don't need to hold onto or defend. If it isn't serving you or supporting your true Who, you can let it go, knowing it was never really yours, and center on what you know to be true.

You can also reassess your commitment to the activity attached to that Who: Do I modify it to bring it into alignment, or is this something that I no longer need in my life? These can be serious and soul-searching questions, but also relieving and clarifying.

We sometimes see people who make major career changes, leave a successful job to go back to school or pursue a less lucrative interest. In most cases they've had the realization that what they were doing was out of alignment with who they were born to be and what they were born to do. Getting in touch with that clarified a new path filled then with deeper meaning and purpose.

It takes a great deal of courage and honesty to face these inconsistencies. But the result is a life of congruence and joy — what I call the authentic you. The difference in the satisfaction and purpose you will experience is tremendous. And others will see you and treat you differently as well.

Golf with a Purpose

You may wonder, "Does my weekly golf outing, distance run or book club have to be connected to my true Who? Isn't that a bit over the top?"

Yes, it is possible to get a little too deep into some of this. But keep in mind that these are things you give your life to, and that ultimately make you you. It may be as simple as they give you the recharge you need to continue to pursue your core passion. Or, they could be an extension of your true Who in a way you hadn't previously considered.

A man I knew, Dean, loved to fly. He owned a plane and flew himself and his family to many different places. But he relished the opportunity to take other people up for flights as often as possible. He would explain all the ins and outs of the airplane, how it flew, all the detailed preparation necessary to make sure it was safe and the pilot was prepared. Once airborne, he would explain the instruments, controls, and switches, and demonstrate how they affected the plane in flight.

But his greatest delight was to have his passenger take the wheel for a few minutes and go through a few controlled maneuvers as he carefully supervised. His delight was contagious, and we always came away with enthusiasm for the miracle of flight. And a love for Dean.

For a long time I thought Dean was just taking us up as another excuse to do what he loved most — fly an airplane. But the more I observed him, I realized he was living consistent with his true Who: he was a gifted teacher. He was passionate about helping others understand complex ideas and find joy and success in them. This was evident in his career. He had been a successful radiologist, but noticed that many of his physician colleagues were terrible money managers and squandered their incomes, mostly through financial ignorance.

Chapter 6 - A Case Study

Rather than continue to read X-Rays all day, (something he found increasingly unfulfilling), he studied and became an expert at financial counseling, particularly for healthcare professionals. He left his radiology practice and worked full time teaching and mentoring doctors in more intelligent and successful money management.

What he did wasn't about money or airplanes. It was about teaching. About seeing people grasp new concepts, master them, build enthusiasm for them, and reap the success. And I don't recall a time when I didn't see Dean with an ear-to-ear smile and enthusiasm bubbling over. He was in total alignment.

So for your weekly golf outing or book club, at the risk of overdoing it, it's at least worth thinking through the activities that take a portion of your life and time, notice any unexplored connections, and understand the purpose and alignment they create.

What's My Who?

Chapter 6 - A Case Study

Chapter 7

So, What's Stopping You?

The Journey to True

Once you understand the exciting power of aligning with your true Who, what's stopping you from making that connection today? Right now?

Maybe the real question is, what's stopping — you? What we don't understand can be what's stopping us. Our own unawareness can be the block to progress. But when our awareness is expanded and our understanding opened — as hopefully yours has been on the journey thus far — suddenly there is a clear path forward.

You've had the mountain top experience. You now see clearly. You are energized and committed, determined to move boldly into this new world of possibilities. You charge ahead with excitement and determination.

But one week in, you find yourself sliding back into the old ways of thinking. And after a few more weeks, the epiphany is a fading memory. It's like it was a nice idea, but nothing really changed.

What's going on? Before judging yourself too harshly, let's take a step back.

Awareness + Rewiring

Let's take another look at what our wonderful subconscious is trying to do. Remember, each of us has miles of neuro-wiring and a big wall to move through in order for our subconscious to keep us safe and consistent in this new mindset. In the meantime, the weight of evidence for the new direction is scant in comparison to years of reinforcing the acquired perception of Who.

So our subconscious is very efficiently doing its job of keeping us consistent with what is believed to be true for possibly many years. Keeping the altered Who aligned with what we think and do, despite the fact that to some extent it's outside of who we really are.

Misalignment With Your True Who

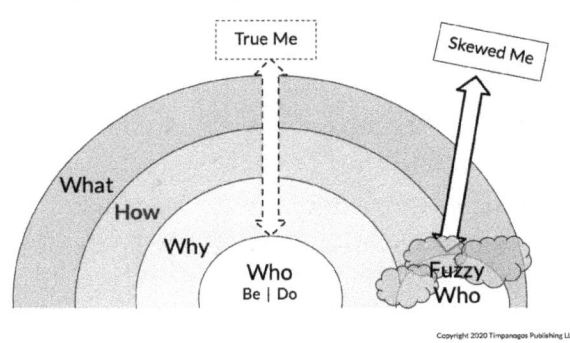

Undo the Untrue

With an understanding of the connection to your true Who, you can begin the process of wiring that image and belief into the subconscious as the one to defend and protect. First, you must get through the wall.

Don't Let Go of Your Who

If this resonated deeply with you, hold onto that vision of yourself. Trust your insight. Bask in it as long as possible.

Our wonderful subconscious is always trying to keep us safe and efficient. We are plowing new ground here, and it's highly likely that before long, your mind will go back to the perception that has been wired in for so many years. It helps to keep this in mind:

As you sit with this clear new view of you, over time it's likely that you will start to hear the naysayer voices — both internally and externally — starting to question what you just discovered. It will likely be thoughts such as:

"That is a crazy idea. How did you think of that?"
"You are daydreaming. Get a grip!"
"There is no way you would be able to do that."
"How could you possibly pay for that, or earn a living doing it?"
"You're too old. That ship has sailed. It's too late."
"Do you know how many other people are trying to do the same thing?"

And on and on and on.

Just realize that none of this changes what you experienced, and what you know to be true. You know what you were born to be. You know what you were born to do. It's your time to step into it completely. Your true Who.

Move Through the Wall

Remember the wall of Shame, Expectation and Gloom? These are tools our mind uses to keep us from straying too far from the status quo, all in the name of keeping us safe. Pushing too hard in a new direction can result in a dose of shame and a feeling of being exposed: "Remember how badly that went for you last time? How disappointed they were?"

The wall of expectation can bring up ideas like: "That's not who you are. You have an image to maintain." And gloomy ideas may bring up thoughts such as: "What would they think of you if you did that? It would be disastrous!"

Pushing On the Wall

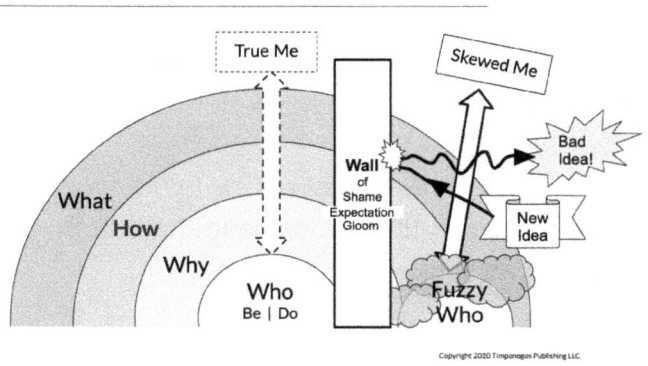

Moving through the wall can seem frustratingly slow and painful. At times you may wonder if any progress is being made at all, Fortunately, there are practices and techniques that can greatly accelerate the process. Three of the most fundamental are:

Approach #1: Let Go

To move forward you must first stop dragging beliefs and thoughts that pull you back. Let go techniques are designed to help you let go of thoughts, beliefs and perceptions that hold you back and limit your ability to move in a new direction. They directly address some of the components of the wall that may be most limiting to you, like shame or comparing yourself to other people.

Forgiveness, gratitude and self-love and acceptance are powerful let go principles that can be very freeing. Each of these encompass a depth of understanding and practice that are well outside of the introductory treatment here.

Many resources are available to help you further explore and apply these approaches in order to further accelerate your progress.[3]

---

[3] See the chapters on gratitude and forgiveness in the author's book *Five Keys to Unlocking the Gift in the Wound*, available on Amazon and Kindle.

Working through these issues can be an epiphany experience in and of itself as you come to recognize skewed beliefs that have held you back, and the freedom afforded by letting them go in favor of greater alignment with your truth.

Approach #2: Empowerment

Empowerment approaches work with the subconscious in wiring new pathways to newly recognized truths that are fully adoptable. These focus on the subconscious propensity for short, concise communication and highly visual images.

Visioning (e.g. vision boards), aspirations or declarations and mindfulness approaches are powerful pathways to subconscious connection and redirection. These techniques, plus a number of others, can be individualized to each person's unique vision and style that keeps them on track and moving forward consistently. Coaching, mentoring and counseling are also strong accelerators in implementing these tools and moving even faster.

I could write many chapters on empowerment techniques and experiences. They truly are powerful and crucial components in the journey to true Who.

However, I have opted not to go into that detail in this book. My hope is that you will catch the vision of the possibilities, search out additional tools and mentors, and light the fire to empower yourself to move rapidly in the true Who direction.

Approach #3: Move In, Embrace

This approach, one of the most effective, also happens to be the most counterintuitive, and therefore the most challenging to implement. Issues that comprise the wall also cause us pain: the pain of shame of not meeting expectations, of failure to live up to an image, of not measuring up or being as good as, of failure and discouragement, among many others.

As humans, we instinctively resist or avoid pain, which means we tend to resist or avoid dealing with these issues that are blocking our progress toward alignment with our true Who. The irony is that the more we resist or avoid, the more the pain intensifies.

The greater irony is that the resolution of the pain lies in the pain itself. Indeed, every wound carries a gift if we have the courage to claim it. The challenge is that the only way to claim the gift is to move into the pain, not away from it. It sounds crazy, and is usually the last thing we want to do. But it is the key to finding the gift that is there waiting, to not only resolving the pain, but finding greater peace, alignment and purpose.

At one point in my career I worked with a partner in jointly developing a program and product that had tremendous potential in helping technical professionals successfully manage their careers. I put nearly two years into creating a truly world class solution. As we began final preparations for launching, he suddenly decided to grab everything we had jointly created and cut me out of the deal. Because of technical and legal details, at the end of the day I was basically left with nothing for my efforts.

I was devastated. I was so angry and frustrated that for months I was caught in a cycle of trying to move away from the experience and move on, but constantly reliving the pain and anger any time I was reminded of or thought about the situation. It was literally eating me up.

Finally, a wise mentor suggested that rather than moving away from the pain, I consider moving into and embracing it, and learning what message or gift it might have for me.

This sounded totally upside down. Why would I accept and move into, much less embrace something that was so excruciating? It made no sense. It wasn't my fault. I didn't deserve this. Why would I want more pain?

Finally, out of desperation, I decided to give it a shot. I sat down and tried thinking about the situation from a different angle: "What's really going on here? What was the purpose, and what's the insight for me? What was my possible role in all this?" As I moved into the pain, showing willingness and crossing that barrier, things suddenly started coming clear through a new insight I had previously been blind to: As brilliant as my partner was, he was afraid. In fact, he was terrified of what might go wrong. I was a variable he couldn't control that might cause something to fail. It was as simple as that.

My perspective shifted. I saw him, and our relationship in a new, truer light. He wasn't a horrible, vindictive person. He was afraid, dealing with demons that caused him to inflict much pain and suffering in others. It was a blind spot, something he was unaware of and unwilling to move into and heal himself. He was a slave to debilitating fear.

That shift changed everything. I was no longer the victim and he the perpetrator. I could accept his fatal human flaw for what it was, and not continue to torture myself with its consequences. I could move on and heal that chapter of my life. The gift of peace was truly life-altering.

To my surprise, the gift didn't stop there. The next layer of insight was even more revealing: "Take a look in the mirror. Check where fear ripples out from you and prevents you from being your best self, and poisons your own relationships." Pow! It hit me right between the eyes. With greater clarity I was able to see my own blind spots more clearly, and realize the effect they had on my alignment with truth. That insight has guided much of my practice in becoming the truest version of me that I can.[4]

Those gifts, won at the price of moving into my wall of pain when everything in me was screaming to run the other way, and being willing to accept what I found there, are priceless indeed. They allow me to move through the wall more effectively and live my true Who more often.

So, here's the counterintuitive invitation: Move into your wall of shame, expectation and gloom that causes

---

[4] See the chapters on The Purpose of Pain and The Pain Portal in the author's book **Five Keys to Unlocking the Gift in the Wound**, available on Amazon and Kindle.

Chapter 7 - So, What's Stopping You?

so much pain. Maybe pick a relationship that is particularly troublesome. Or a resentment about shaming from a parent, teacher, sibling or caretaker. Or a nagging belief that you somehow don't measure up.

Move Into Pain - Find the Gift

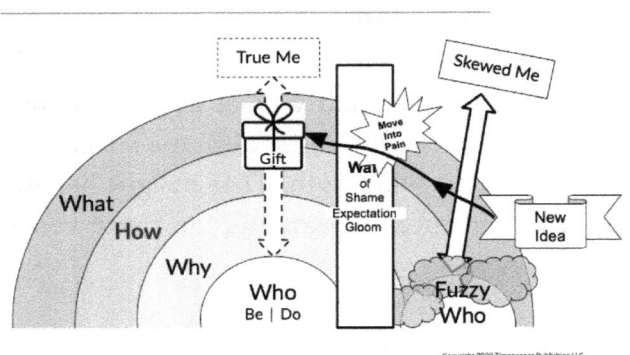

Move into the wall to move through it. Don't fight it, push against, try to break it down. Move into it. You'll come out the other side holding a priceless gift and standing closer to your true Who than you ever thought possible.

Consistency

Creating a new, safe place where your rediscovered Who can thrive takes time, repetition and patience. When you think about it, if it were as easy as, "gain new insight, change beliefs and behavior to align," you would have already done it, right? The process of rewiring your internal watchguard to a new comfort zone requires consistent, patient practice and encouragement.

While it can seem painfully long, slow and discouraging at times, you're usually doing better than you think you are. And when you look from where you stand back to where you started, even modest progress can be monumental.

So, Do I Quit My Job?

You could have potentially life changing experiences with a rediscovered Who. Perhaps you've been slogging through, putting in time at a job or relationship or situation that's become increasingly tedious and unfulfilling. Or maybe a life stage or experience created the opportunity for reevaluating life, and a yearning for something more keeps popping up. Rediscovering a born-to-be insight can be hugely liberating — and scary at the same time.

If your purpose takes you in a new direction, do you just up and quit and strike out? You may wonder, "I'm so excited about this new insight, but where do I start?

Chapter 7 - So, What's Stopping You?

How do I tackle something that's in my comfort zone of inner passion, but way out of my comfort zone in knowing how to go about making it a reality?"

These are actually questions about How and What. With a clear Who and strong Why, your mind can get to work on how to best go about it and what the possible outcomes will be. This is where it gets really fun.

With alignment, the subconscious mind, conscious mind and inspiration start working together in powerful new ways. You may find that you're:

- More passionate
- More creative and insightful
- More committed
- More open to inspiration - more faithful, prayerful or contemplative
- More tuned in to unique gifts and talents

You may find paths opening that you hadn't seen or considered before. People or relationships may pop up that weren't on your radar previously. Ideas and impressions may come to you with new directions or approaches to take.

You will have put into motion the machinery to bring into your life what you were born to be and what you were born to do on this planet.

A friend of mine worked for many years as a successful chef and TV personality, and later online channel personality. He did well for himself, had a wide circle of friends and associates, a great family and fulfilling personal life. But later in his career, he had a yearning to do more, to have a greater direct impact on people's lives. Cooking brought people together and built great relationships and friendships — something he treasured. But he had a sense there was something more.

Through a number of experiences and by observing his own interests, he discovered a passion for coaching and working with people who deal with identity challenges. He realized he not only had the passion, but also the talent to be highly effective and touch many lives for good.

He was inspired with this idea and wanted to train and fully certify as a life coach and start transitioning to a new life path. But it needed to be a vocation, not a hobby. His passion led him to a series of introductions and later relationships that opened the opportunity for a certification program that fit perfectly with his direction and values. However, the cost was prohibitive for his financial situation.

Chapter 7 - So, What's Stopping You?

But he continued to pursue it, looking for different options to make it work. One day, a conversation with the program director uncovered a mutual need. A series of upcoming training programs would require catering and food services for attendees. My friend needed a way to cover his tuition, and happened to be a chef with years of catering experience. A match was made and my friend was on his way to truly living his Who.

So to answer the original question: you don't necessarily need to quit your job to pursue your born-to-be. Get the trifecta of subconscious, conscious and inspiration working on helping you live your purpose, and follow the paths that open.

What's My Who?

Chapter 7 - So, What's Stopping You?

Chapter 8

Unshakable Who + Heart of a Lion

Our Who can never be taken from us. How and What can change, be destroyed, foiled, spoiled, run aground. But none of that changes our true Who. It can never be taken. Only given up.

Terrible things don't shake us when our thoughts are firmly wired to our Who. Divorce, job loss, insults, illness, natural disasters, government upheaval...can all change our What, our circumstances, or our How, how we go about gaining and defending them. But none of these change our core Who. It is constant regardless of what else happens.

That's the good news. The flip side is also true. When holding onto an altered Who, we embrace and spend our lives defending someone else's Who, someone else's life direction.

When the "Who" is fuzzy and fluid, one will be shell-shocked and shaken with every change in What or How — every change in circumstance. Much of the stress experienced in life is tied to expectations for things that in truth, don't really matter at the true Who level.

Heart of a Lion

Several years ago I was enrolled in elite mentor training, and was put into a mastermind group with a woman named Penny. Our group met weekly for training with our coach, accountability for our action step commitments, and sharing successes and insights.

Our group really gelled, to the point that all of us were able to move into being open with each other in a way that was healthy and insightful. After the first few meetings a clear picture of Penny started to emerge.

She was in a comfortable financial position, but felt an internal drive to help people live healthier lives by learning to deal with the emotional, mindset and physical aspects of obesity and all its downstream effects. She had suffered greatly in many up and down cycles over a number of years herself, and had developed an approach that was proving to be highly effective. Her great desire was to mentor individuals or groups in reclaiming their lives from the ravages of these challenges.

Over time I recognized that Penny lived the dichotomy of knowing her Who and feeling its passion, but struggling with the walls and programming that told her she wasn't enough, couldn't do it, didn't measure up. I marveled at her knowledge, quality of content and love of and commitment to people. And I shared her pain as I watched the struggle with speaking, presenting and contacting. Despite her competence, she often shared doubts about her ability: "Why would anyone come to my classes? They wouldn't learn anything new. I would probably stumble all over my words. Somebody else is probably already teaching this stuff anyway." The negative thought battle was on full display.

But Penny never gave up. She did all the assignments, exercises and follow-ups completely and on time. She took extra training and classes. She sought and acted on feedback and suggestions. She worked hard and sincerely cared.

At one point a family situation placed a great burden on her physically, emotionally and time-wise. It would have been very easy for her to put everything on hold and focus solely on her change in circumstance. Yet she still continued to be the one leading out on the learning and practices that would make the most difference. She wouldn't let go of her dream.

Penny is a heart-of-a-lion person. It takes great courage to consistently fight all the resistance to a true Who — to live true to that core despite the internal struggles and changes in circumstances. To continue to get up and try again when things don't work out.

Penny finally launched her program. She started with one class, then another and another. Today she is helping hundreds of people find hope and success where there was previously only despair. She is confident, enthusiastic and energetic. She finds alignment, gives her gift, and experiences the joy of living her born-to-be.

True to True Who

The journey to alignment with our true Who is a heart-of-a-lion quest. It starts with the courage to consider rediscovering our authentic self, clouded by expectations and beliefs that aren't even our own. And it ends with alignment to that newfound realty, and the tranquility, purpose and joy that accompany it.

In between is a lot of struggle, confusion and halting progress as we sort through how to make our newly clarified vision a consistent reality. That's the heart-of-a-lion part.

That's when the people who actually do change their lives and change the world step out and claim their authentic place on the stage with confidence and unapologetic conviction — unafraid of being labeled the crazy ones, the misfits and the dreamers. Confident that being a compassionate healer, insightful teacher or guide to identity is enough, because that is truly who they were born to be.

It is enough for any of us.

Now it is your turn. You were born to be.

Chapter 8 – Unshakable Who + Heart of a Lion

Epilogue

So, What's *My* Who?

Many people ask me, "So, wha*t's your* Who? You've talked a lot about what other people discovered. But what did *you* discover?"

As I've walked this wonderful rediscovery journey, I've come to understand a few core principles that have helped me to first clarify and embrace my Who, and then to consistently practice living true to what I've rediscovered. Here are the three key principles:

Key 1: Quick Clarity

Unlike grappling with my Why, my Who coalesced quickly and almost effortlessly when I rediscovered what was going on inside my mind and heart.

Once I made the space to accept it, it truly was a 'coming home' type experience; something I knew had always been there, piled under layers of assumptions and expectations, just waiting to be owned. As I wrote and drew pictures, the image of my Who took center stage in profound simplicity.

At one point I stepped back and said, "This *is* who I am. This *is* who I was born to be, and what I was born to do.

It just *is*." It was such a relief to understand my true core. A floodgate opened inside of me, and the desires and direction in my life to that point finally made sense.

There are people who insist that this rediscovery is a much longer, evolutionary process that fleshes out over time; that it can't be as simple as going inward with a few simple experiences and coming away knowing your Who.

My experience is that rediscovering the initial insight as to who you truly are is a rather quick, profound experience if you approach it with an open, curious and accepting mindset. Much of what impedes this process is fear of our own brilliance. Marianne Williamson put it this way:

"Our deepest fear is that we are powerful beyond measure. It is our light, not our darkness that most frightens us. We ask ourselves, 'Who am I to be brilliant, gorgeous, talented, fabulous?"

Much of our programming teaches us that confidently claiming who we are is somehow not humble, not possible, that we aren't worthy or don't measure up. That we're an imposter (known as imposter syndrome). It is these types of fears that make many people question what they are sensing or what they know to be true. They are afraid to claim and own their Who, and instead get distracted with doubts that suggest it must be more difficult and complicated to unravel, and will take much more time. They bury it, seek other's opinions and avoid the discussion.

Think about it. If Steve Jobs had doubted his 'crazy ones' mantra, and waited until later to unravel it and claim it, Apple as we know it probably wouldn't exist today.

Your Who is ready and available for you to fully claim. Don't let fear and doubt rob you of that opportunity.

Key 2: Levels of Evolution

The second question is: does your Who evolve or morph over time as you grow and mature and have different life experiences. Does it move different directions as you move different directions?
I believe that the understanding of your Who includes a number of levels or depths. So it does evolve, but in a different way than we may typically think about.

The first insight is most likely the first level. While hugely beneficial, this insight will likely be followed by additional levels of understanding and depth that will further clarify life direction, and will likely also fit new opportunities and ways to express your Who.

But the core purpose probably hasn't changed. It has just been enlightened and fleshed out with additional levels of understanding that illuminate paths and opportunities for expression that are still tied to your true Who.

There is always another level. This is how it evolves, vs. changing directions or basic characteristics. In my case, the initial insight was simple and clear, and has stayed consistent throughout the evolution. What has changed is my level of understanding and detailed insights regarding what my Who means to me as I work through the How and What.

Key 3: Living My Who

This is the part that requires focus, a lot of processing, a lot of commitment and a lot of effort. This is the constant, almost daily rewiring to accept the changes required to adopt the newly rediscovered true me.

A friend described it as almost a 'Groundhog Day' type experience of daily effort that can at times seem hopelessly tiring. Through many cycles of forward and backward stepping, I've found these practices to be most effective:

- Keep the vision bright. Never let go of what you have rediscovered to be true. This is the heart-of-a-lion mantra discussed earlier, and is vastly strengthened by visioning techniques.

- Use the let go and empowerment techniques described in chapter 7. They are immensely helpful if implemented as a consistent part of your daily practice.

- Embrace the pain. I can't overemphasize the importance of this concept. Most of the fear and the pain caused by fear is best addressed by moving into it, understanding its purpose, and receiving its message and gift for us. Once you master this counterintuitive approach, things can really start to accelerate. My journey down this path is captured in my previous book *Five Keys to Unlocking the Gift in the Wound*.

So, What's My Who?

With that background, I share my first level Who. I do so with the intent of living true to what I have rediscovered, which includes writing books like this one and interacting with honest truth seekers like you.

Epilogue

My Who:

"I am a rock in the storm."

Over the years, many people have commented to me that I inspire immediate trust. That I am a good listener. That I share wisdom, calm and encouragement, particularly during troubled times. That I am able to help them find peace and direction in the storm.

I have come to understand that this is the manifestation of my Who. That's who I am, what I am really good at, and what I am passionate about.

There are many additional levels of detail and insight beyond this initial simple idea. But that Who continues to be my guiding star in how I move forward into many new and interesting opportunities in life.

Why Not You? Why Not Now?

Wherever you are, you *can* rediscover Who you were born to be, and What you were born to do. Now is the time. The world needs the authentic, powerful gifts only you own.

Be willing to give yourself permission to consider the question burning in you:

What's My Who?

About Mark L. Dayton

My What

I serve as an author, speaker, business executive, mentor and entrepreneur. My career includes executive positions with companies from Fortune 100 to startups, and spans multiple industries and locations. More recently I am involved in writing, coaching, training, and advising a trauma intervention humanitarian organization.

My How

I combine a passion for unlocking human potential with a knack for clear, engaging communication to provide books, training and mentoring that helps individuals and organizations become all they were meant to be.

Published books include *The Phase 3 Fulcrum, 5 Keys to Unlocking the Gift in the Wound*, *Frederick's Christmas Concert,* and *What's My Who?*

My Why   I inspire people with hope, humor, wisdom and the heart of a lion to rediscover, accept and live Who they were born to be and What they were born to do to become their truest and finest selves.

My Who   My Level 1 Who is: "I am a rock in the storm."

www.ingramcontent.com/pod-product-compliance
Lightning Source LLC
Chambersburg PA
CBHW070852050426
42453CB00012B/2152